know God
Published by Orange, a division of The reThink Group, Inc.
5870 Charlotte Lane, Suite 300
Cumming, GA 30040 U.S.A.
The Orange logo is a registered trademark of The reThink Group, Inc.

Other Orange products are available online and direct from the publisher. Visit our website at www.WhatIsOrange.org for more resources like these.

ISBN: 978-1-941259-75-7

©2016 The reThink Group, Inc.

reThink Conceptual Team:
Ben Crawshaw, Kristen Ivy, Reggie Joiner, Cara Martens, Dan Scott
Lead Writer: Lauren Terrell
Editing Team: Lauren Makahon, Jennifer Wilder
Project Manager: Nate Brandt
Art Direction: Ryan Boon
Design: FiveStone

Printed in the United States of America
Second Edition 2016

1 2 3 4 5 6 7 8 9 10

09/15/16

A 28-DAY DEVOTIONAL EXPERIENCE FOR KIDS

KNOW
GOD

START HERE

DON'T READ THIS BOOK.

Okay, read it.
But don't *just* read it.

Write in it. Draw on it. Mark it up.

AND

Find a grown-up you can talk to about it.

Think of one person you know who loves God.
(Make sure it's someone you feel really comfortable talking to.)

Are you thinking of someone?
(Hint: It could be your mom, dad, teacher, small group leader or coach.)

Okay, here's the most important thing you will do with this book:

TEAR OUT
THIS PAGE $\longrightarrow$

. . . and give it to that person.

That person is going to go through this experience with you because it will be *so* much better than just thinking about these things alone.

Dear _____,

I just got a journal called *know God*. It's all about how to get to **know God** better. I wanted to tell you about it first because you **know God**. And even though this is a pretty cool book, it won't be able to tell me everything I need to know about knowing God. So, I thought it would be fun if we could talk about it together.

This journal has devotions for 28 days. That's 4 weeks. I'm not sure I will be able to do every single day, but I want to. Do you think you could help remind me to stick with it?

And one more thing: At the end of each week, could we get together just to talk through what I'm learning? I might have some questions. There are even some things that you could ask me when we get together. (They are on the back of this page. But I'm not going to read them yet. I'll just wait and be surprised when you ask.)

Thank you for your influence in my life. I'm excited about the next four weeks together.

Sincerely,

_____

Hanging out with you is always fun. I'm excited for the next four weeks. Anytime we get together, feel free to ask me things like:

What's the most interesting thing you read this week?
Was there something you had a question about?

But more specifically: Here's what I'm going to be reading, and what we might want to talk about.

WEEK ONE

This week I discovered that in order to **know God** more, we need to **HEAR** from God. I learned to . . .
. . . listen to what God has made.
. . . listen to what Jesus said.
. . . listen to God's Word.
. . . listen to God's Word everyday.
. . . listen to God's Word by memorizing it.
. . . listen to God's Spirit.

When we get together this week, ask me . . .
What did you read in the Bible this week? How did it help you **know God** more? What was difficult to understand?

WEEK TWO

This week I discovered that in order to **know God** more, we need to **PRAY** to God.
By looking at The Lord's Prayer, I learned that I should . . .
. . . pray alone.
. . . pray to a God who knows me.
. . . pray with gratitude.
. . . pray with honesty.
. . . pray for my needs.
. . . pray for forgiveness.
. . . pray continually.

When we get together this week, ask me . . .
When are you most likely to pray?
What is the hardest part about prayer for you?

WEEK THREE

This week I discovered that in order to **know God** more, we need to **TALK** about God. I learned the importance of . . .
. . . talking with people who believe in Jesus.
. . . talking about who God is.
. . . talking about what God says.
. . . talking about my doubts and questions.
. . . talking about what God has done.
. . . talking about what God is doing.
. . . talking with anyone who asks.

When we get together this week, ask me . . .
Who (besides me) do you feel comfortable talking with about your relationship with God?
What is one thing you see God has done in your life or in someone else's life?

WEEK FOUR

This week I discovered that as we get to **know God** more, we will want to **LIVE** a life that honors Him. I learned that every day I can worship God when I . . .
. . . honor God with love.
. . . honor God with praise.
. . . honor God with obedience.
. . . honor God with generosity.
. . . honor God with serving.
. . . honor God with my work.
. . . honor God with rest.

When we get together this week, ask me . . .
What is one way you want to honor God more?
Now that you've finished this devotional, how can I help you keep getting to **know God** more every week?

KNOWING GOD IS
KIND OF LIKE
KNOWING ANYONE
ELSE—YOU CAN LEARN
A LOT ABOUT THEM
AND STILL
BE SURPRISED
BY THEM.

HOW DO I KNOW GOD?

Knowing God doesn't happen in a moment. It's not like you wake up one morning and *BAM*, you **know God**. All about God. Everything there is to know. No more questions. No more doubts. No more what ifs or how comes.

In fact, if you were to talk to some people who believe in God and have loved Him for a long time, they would probably tell you they're still learning new things about God. They probably still have a few questions. Go ahead—ask them. See what they say.

Knowing God is kind of like knowing anyone else—
you can learn a lot about them and still be surprised by them.

Knowing God isn't like solving a puzzle.

It's a
Laugh-out-loud,
frustrating,
catch-you-off-guard,
exciting relationship.

So beware: you can read every word in this book, fill in every blank, follow every suggestion, and still not know *all* there is to know about God.

But that's okay. This book isn't about knowing all you need to know. It's about helping you start an adventure. It's an adventure to . . .

> . . . learn new things.
> . . . unlearn what you thought you knew.
> . . . connect with a God who already loves you more than you will ever understand.

But before you go any further—before you even turn to the next page—there is one thing you absolutely must know about knowing God.

If you want to **know God**, start with Jesus.

Yeah, yeah, you might have guessed that's where you need to begin. But really, Jesus is the place to start. Why? Well, because Jesus is God. But Jesus was also a Man. He was born. He had a mother. He had birthdays. We don't know how He celebrated them, but He had them. He ate, slept, went to the bathroom. He was God, living on earth like you and me. So what He said, yeah, those are God's words. And what He did, well, that should give us a pretty good idea of what God is like.

So**, if you really want to get to know God, get to know Jesus.**

HOW DO I KNOW JESUS?

That's the next question, right? Jesus promised to be with us all of the time, but we can't see Him like we see our friends. Jesus isn't exactly sending you a text or calling you on the phone. So, how are you supposed to get to know Him?

If you want to know Jesus, read His Story.

In case you missed that, Jesus' story is the Bible. Maybe you have a Bible that someone gave you a long time ago, or maybe you search the Internet so you can find a funny Bible story about donkeys. Other than looking up a verse or answering a question at church, what do you really know about the Bible?

You may not know this, but the Bible is not a book. Sure, it looks like a book. You can flip through it like a book. But it's really not just one book.

It's 66 books,
Written by over 40 authors
Over 1,600 years.
And it all comes together to tell ONE STORY.

It's not just any story. It's a story about:
A really BIG God who loved people
SO MUCH
He became a human—Jesus.

Jesus
Lived,
Died,
And rose again . . .

So WE could
Be forgiven
Redeemed
And live with Him forever.

This is the story that helps us get to know Jesus.

This is the story that helps us understand everything we know about God.

⊙ HERE ARE A FEW THINGS WE KNOW ABOUT GOD BECAUSE OF HIS STORY:

» We know God is good because God created a magnificent heaven.

» We know bad things will happen because when people broke God's rule, the world was broken.

» We know that God won't abandon us, because we see how God still loved disobedient and sinful people over thousands of years.

» We know we can trust God to keep His promises, because He already kept the greatest promise by sending His Son, Jesus.

» We know we can be forgiven, because Jesus died for us and already took on all the punishment for our sin.

» We know that one day we can live with God in heaven because Jesus defeated death once and for all.

» We know that until that time, we are meant to live a life full of love that follows what Jesus taught.

THE BIG IDEA.

Let's make sure you are following along so far. You want to **know God**? Great!

Start by getting to know Jesus. And the best way to know Jesus is to read His Story. The Bible. Specifically, the part where He shows up on the scene.

In other words, start reading in the Gospels (Matthew, Mark, Luke, John).

There you can read all about what Jesus did and what Jesus said.

But even before you read the Gospels, you might be interested to know there is one thing Jesus *did* that is more important than anything else.

You can probably guess what it is. More than likely, it's the reason you have this book. You know: Jesus died for the sins of the world, and after three days He was raised from the dead.

That's the most important thing.

But did you also know there is one thing Jesus *said* that is more important than anything else He said? It's true. Of all the things Jesus said, there is one thing that's the key to understanding everything you will ever know about God. It's actually like the decoder to understanding all the rest.

Jesus said this one thing, on a day when a group of religious leaders—men who had spent their entire lives studying God—came up to Him and one of them asked Him this question:

"Which is the most important commandment in the law?"

Check out what Jesus said:

" 'Love the Lord your God with all your heart and with all your soul and with all your mind.' This is the first and greatest commandment. And the second is like it: 'Love your neighbor as yourself.' All the Law and the Prophets hang on these two commandments" (Matthew 22:37-40).

That's it.
The most important commandment.
The BIGGEST idea.

Everything else that the Bible teaches about how you should live comes back to this. If you start to understand these 48 words now, you can worry about the other hundreds of thousands of words in the Bible later.

Because really, it's pretty simple.
The most important thing you could ever do is to LOVE GOD.

And if you aren't sure how to love God, maybe the best test is to start by loving the people God loves. God loves you. God loves others.

You can know for sure that God loves you because He created you and He cared enough to show up on this planet to die for you so you could be forgiven and be with Him forever.

And you can know for sure that God loves others because, guess what, He created them and died for them, too. All of them.

It's like Jesus summed up everything you need to know by saying: *It's about three relationships. God. You. Others.*

Or if you want to simplify it even more, it's about one idea.

LOVE.

Love God.
Love yourself the way He loves you.
Love others the way He loves them.

That's pretty much the most important thing Jesus said. So on your adventure to **know God**, it's a good place to start.

WE ARE LIVING
OUT OUR STORY AS WE
LEARN TO LOVE EACH
OTHER THE WAY THAT
GOD LOVES.

TO SUM IT ALL UP

1

When you get to know
GOD'S STORY
it not only helps you
know more about
God, it helps you
understand your own
story. You know more
about yourself because
you understand more
about the One who
made you.

2

And as you
understand how
YOUR STORY
fits with God's greater
Story, you will learn to
see how you are
connected to the
stories of others.

3

We are living out
OUR STORY
as we learn to love
each other the way
that God loves.

SEE HOW THAT WORKS?

4 WAYS TO KNOW GOD . . .

EVEN THOUGH THERE'S NO FORMULA FOR KNOWING ALL YOU NEED TO KNOW ABOUT GOD, THERE ARE A FEW THINGS YOU CAN DO EVERY DAY THAT WILL HELP YOU GET TO KNOW GOD MORE.

HEAR

If you want to get to know someone, what's one of the first things you do? You listen.

That person is the only one who can tell you what he is thinking and feeling—what makes him laugh, what makes him angry. The same is true for God. If you want to know God, you have to learn how to listen. You have to get in the habit of hearing from Him. And when you listen to God, it helps you learn to *trust* Him more.

PRAY

Have you ever been in a conversation where the other person did *all* the talking? That's lame. And guess what? God thinks so, too. He doesn't want a relationship with you where He's the only one talking. He wants you to talk back. He wants to hear from you—your frustrations, your worries, your fears, and your interests. So, if you want to know God, get in the habit of talking with Him. Because when you pray, it helps you *connect* with God.

THAT'S WHAT THIS JOURNAL IS REALLY ALL ABOUT: FOUR THINGS THAT YOU CAN DO TODAY (AND EVERY DAY) THAT WILL HELP YOU KNOW GOD.

Who is your closest friend? Do you talk about that person—even when they're not around? Sure, you do. You talk about what they did. You talk about what they said. You talk about what you plan to do with them tomorrow. You probably also like hanging around other people who know your friend, and like to talk about your friend with them, too. The same is true with God. As you get to know Him more, you will find that you want to talk about Him more. You want to be around other people who talk about Him, too. And when you talk about Him, and listen to others talk about Him, it will help you *see* God in new ways.

Have you ever had someone give you a gift or do something for you that was so unbelievably stinking amazing that you just *had* to find a way to thank them? You already know that God has done something amazing for you—He sent His Son to die so you could be forgiven—but as you get to know God more, you will find out new things about how awesome He is. Don't be surprised if you find yourself suddenly wanting to sing or paint or play an instrument as a way to show God how amazing He is. Or maybe that's not your thing. Maybe you will want to run a mile or climb to the top of a mountain. You might start loving and doing things for others more. No matter how you do it, the more you spend time with God, the more you will want to *honor* God in big and small ways.

WEEK 1

HEAR

HEAR

If you want to **know God**, the first thing to do is hear from Him. But how do you hear from Someone who isn't likely to . . .
. . . show up to your school?
. . . sit next to you at the lunch table?
. . . send you a text?
. . . write you a note in science class?

How can you hear from Someone if you can't even see Him?

Actually, the Bible gives us a pretty good clue. It says:

> **"No one has ever seen God, but the one and only Son, who is himself God and is in closest relationship with the Father, has made him known" (John 1:18).**

God's one and only Son. Jesus. There it is again, this idea that **if you want to know God, you should get to know Jesus.**

Jesus is the best way to **know God** because He spent time living on this planet. And while He was here, He spent a lot of time with twelve guys who are sometimes called disciples and sometimes called apostles. Whatever you want to call them, they got to know Jesus pretty well.

They were there when Jesus taught.
They were there when Jesus worked miracles.
They were there when Jesus died . . .
. . . and they saw Him alive again after He rose from the dead.

They were also around when Jesus ascended. That means one minute He was standing on a hill with His disciples saying goodbye, and the next minute He rose up into the sky and disappeared. Pretty wild, huh? But it's all in the Bible. You can read more about it in Acts 1.

So, why does it matter that these twelve guys witnessed so much of Jesus' life and teachings? And what does that have to do with **hearing from God**?

A lot.

"You will be my witnesses in Jerusalem, and in all Judea and Samaria, and to the ends of the earth" (Acts 1:8).

Right before Jesus ascended, He gave them the most important mission:

"You will be my witnesses in Jerusalem, and in all Judea and Samaria, and to the ends of the earth" (Acts 1:8).

Jesus wanted his disciples, apostles, friends to go tell people what they had seen and heard.

And guess what?
They did.
They went. They told. Some of them wrote it down.

In fact, two of Jesus' disciples, Matthew and John, wrote down stories from the time they spent with Jesus. Remember, these guys knew Jesus. He was their Friend. When they wrote about Jesus, they were writing about Someone they had traveled with, eaten with, and hung out with. They had seen Him in action.

They wrote about how He was born. They wrote about how His ministry got started. They wrote about what He did and what He said.

Two other guys, Mark and Luke, also wrote about Jesus. They weren't disciples who hung out with Jesus, but they knew some of those guys. Mark was friends with Peter (another disciple), and Luke interviewed just about everyone who met Jesus.

Today, you can still read the words of Matthew, Mark, Luke and John in the Bible. They are the first four books of the New Testament. We call these four books the Gospels, and each one gives us a unique look at the life of Jesus.

If you want to know God, read His Story. Think about who He is and what He says. Hearing from God in this way will help you trust Him more. So here's one thing to think about as you get started this week: **if you want to know God, remember His words**.

DAY 1

Freeze! Look around you. Where are you? (Please don't say your bathroom.) Are you somewhere you can smell fresh air, hear the wind in the trees and feel the grass prickle your feet? No?! Well, grab your Bible, a pen and this book and find a quiet place outside to read today's devotion. (Unless outside is too cold, rainy, dark, or full of life-threatening tornadoes . . . in that case, find a quiet—and safe—place inside where you can at least *see* outside.)

I'll wait . . .

Great! Doesn't that view beat the smell of last week's gym socks?

❷ NOW THAT YOU'RE SETTLED, LET ME ASK YOU A COUPLE OF QUESTIONS. WHO IS YOUR FAVORITE MUSIC GROUP?

....

❷ WHO IS YOUR FAVORITE AUTHOR?

....

How did you decide on these favorites? By listening to the music and reading the stories they made!

Take a look around. You are *surrounded* by what God has made. And just like you learn more about your favorite music group by listening to the songs they made, you can learn more about God by listening to what He has made.

But before you take a stethoscope to the nearest tree, let's talk about what it really means to *listen* to God's creation. Psalm 19:1 says,

> *"The heavens declare the glory of God; the skies proclaim the work of his hands."*

In other words, when you look at the great big sky that God made with its bright blues, deep purples, and soft pinks, when you see bright rays of sun shooting through stark white clouds, it's almost as if the whole sky has come together to show you how massive, creative, beautiful and powerful God is.

And it's not just the sky! The humongous oak tree speaks of God's strength; the shade found beneath its branches tells of His shelter. The warm sun radiates His love to all corners of the earth while the cool moon shines His light in the darkness.

Everything God has made tells us something about who God is. So if you want to know God, start by **listening to what God has made.**

◐ LOOK AROUND YOU. FIND FIVE THINGS THAT GOD HAS MADE. LIST THOSE THINGS HERE:

1.
....
2.
....
3.
....
4.
....
5.
....

◐ WHAT DO YOU THINK SOME OF THOSE THINGS MIGHT SHOW YOU ABOUT GOD?

....

....

....

HEAR

DAY 2

◉ WHO IS THE BEST FRIEND YOU'VE EVER HAD?

....

◉ WRITE THE STORY OF HOW YOU MET YOUR BEST FRIEND AND WHAT MADE YOU TWO CLICK:

....

....

....

Whether your best friend is a kid you met at school or your pet hamster, Louie, it's probably safe to say you got along because you have something in common. Maybe you both love sports. Maybe you share a fear of spiders. Maybe you also enjoy frantically running on a giant wheel.

Bottom line is, you're best friends because you had conversations, spent time together and got to know each other.

So how can you be friends with God when you can't see or hear Him? How can you get to know Someone who can't play soccer or scream at spiders with?

That's where Jesus comes in. Jesus *is* God. He can play soccer. He can squeal at spiders. And most importantly, when Jesus was on earth He spoke God's words, telling us what God is all about. In Matthew 7:24 and 26, Jesus says,

> *"Therefore everyone who hears these words of mine and puts them into practice is like a wise man who built his house on the rock. . . . But everyone who hears these words of mine and does not put them into practice is like a foolish man who built his house on sand."*

If you want to get to know God, **listen to what Jesus said.** Put His words into practice and just like a house built on rock will still be standing after a bad storm, you can stand strong no matter what is thrown your way.

Jesus said some pretty amazing things—things that tell us how we should live. Find a big rock (or a few smaller ones) outside and rinse them off. Once they're dry, find a permanent marker and carefully write one of these Scripture references on each rock:

» Mark 10:43-45   » Matthew 5:16
» Luke 12:22   » Matthew 6:19-21
» Mark 12:30-31

Look up these five passages of Scripture in your Bible. These are all words Jesus actually spoke! If you have a Bible app or can find a Bible online, try reading them each in different versions. You might even ask your mom or dad or someone you trust to help you find a good translation to start with.

WHAT DO THESE WORDS STRAIGHT FROM GOD'S MOUTH MEAN TO YOU?

....

HOW COULD THEY HELP YOU AVOID TROUBLE?

....

HOW COULD THEY HELP YOU BECOME MORE LIKE JESUS?

....

WHAT DO THEY TELL YOU ABOUT WHO GOD IS?

....

DAY 3

Imagine this: You're flying in a small two-person jet—just you and the pilot—when the pilot suddenly passes out. You've never flown a plane before, but somehow, you manage to grab the right gears and push the right buttons to land the plane. Unfortunately, the pilot doesn't survive the crash and you find yourself alone on a deserted island with no contact with the rest of the world.

Okay, okay, I just described the first chapter of the popular novel, *Hatchet*. You might not have read it yet, but let's just *say* you lived through the same experience. What three items would you want to have with you to be equipped to survive in this deserted island?

1.
....
2.
....
3.
....

Hopefully, you won't find yourself in that situation anytime soon, but I bet you've had a problem you didn't feel equipped to handle. Your friend says something mean about you. Your parents are fighting. You are moving. Second Timothy 3:16-17 says,

> *"All scripture is God-breathed and is useful for teaching, rebuking, correcting and training in righteousness, so that the man of God may be thoroughly equipped for every good work."*

Basically, no matter the situation, Scripture—the Bible—can help. Every single word is meant to help you, someone who loves God and follows Jesus, be equipped for whatever life throws your way! That's why it's important to **listen to God's Word**.

So what's the first step to listening to God's Word? **Get it**. No, really. Go out and get a Bible. And if you already have a Bible, make sure it's a version you can read and understand. Remember: you can ask someone to help you find a good version that will be easy for you to understand.

Start listening to God's Word so the next time you find yourself in a sticky situation, you're equipped with the Scripture to carry you through—unless, of course, you're stranded on a deserted island. In that case, you might also want to be equipped with a hatchet.

◎ DO YOU ALREADY HAVE A BIBLE?

      YES   NO

◎ IF YES, WHAT DO YOU LIKE ABOUT THE BIBLE YOU HAVE?

....

....

◎ WHAT DO YOU NOT LIKE?

....

◎ DO SOME RESEARCH AND WRITE THE NAME OF A FEW BIBLES THAT YOU THINK YOU MIGHT LIKE TO HAVE. (TIP: START BY LOOKING UP BIBLES FOR KIDS AND TEENS.)

....

....

....

◎ NOW, SHOW YOUR WISH LIST TO A PARENT AND FIGURE OUT A WAY TO GET GOD'S WORD!

DAY 4

Where is the darkest place in your house? A closet? A bathroom? Grab a flashlight and find your way to that room now.

You there?

Great! Now turn the lights off and the flashlight on for the rest of today's reading.

In July 2012, a massive power outage affected northern India leaving over 620 million people without electricity! We aren't talking about a flicker that makes you reset your clocks. We're talking 620 million people—one out of every ten people in the world—with no light, no public transportation, no microwaves, fridges, or stoves. And the blackout lasted for three days in some areas!

That's a lot of people wandering around in the dark, unable to see where they're going! Whether you've seen a power outage or not, you can probably understand the feeling of not knowing where you're going. But Psalm 119:105 says,

"Your word is a lamp to my feet a light for my path."

Now, that's not to say if more people carried Bibles in northern India that summer, 600 million stubbed toes and bruised shins would have been prevented. God's Word is a different kind of light entirely.

We're all on a path. The choices we make, the people we surround ourselves with and how we react to life's challenges all determine where that path leads. But if we **listen to God's Word**, we can see where our path will take us—as if we were holding a flashlight. The Bible can tell us if our choices are going to take us down an easy path or a difficult one. And when we find ourselves in the dark on a path we never meant to go down, God's Word can lead us back to a better one.

So now that you have a Bible—one you can read and understand—start listening to what God's Word has to say.

Think about your own path:

○ WHO ARE THE PEOPLE YOU HANG OUT WITH EACH DAY? NAME JUST A FEW.

1.
....

2.
....

3.
....

○ ARE THOSE PEOPLE MAKING WISE CHOICES? HOW DO YOU KNOW?

....

....

○ WHAT ARE SOME OF THE CHOICES THAT YOU HAVE TO MAKE EVERY DAY THAT COULD AFFECT WHAT YOUR LIFE LOOKS LIKE IN THE FUTURE? (Example: who you sit with at lunch, what you say about your teacher etc . . .)

....

....

....

If you have an index in the back of your Bible or a Bible app, use it to look up certain topics and hear what God's Word has to say about the things you're facing right now.

HEAR

DAY 5

Cross your arms.

Did you cross them right over left or left over right?

Interlace your fingers.

Is your right thumb on top of your left or the other way around?

Jump five times on your left foot while waving your arms.

(That last one was just to see if you'd do it.)

Some habits—like crossing your arms—come so naturally that you don't even think about them. Others, like brushing your teeth or washing your hands, don't come so easily. And then there are the ones like picking your nose or biting your toenails that *shouldn't* come so easily . . .

But today isn't about *breaking* habits. It's about *making* habits.

In the Old Testament, the first psalm in the book of Psalms starts out with,

> *"Blessed is the man who does not walk in the counsel of the wicked. . . . But his delight is in the law of the Lord, on his law he meditates day and night" (Psalm 1:1-2).*

What do *you* think about all day and night? If you answered "God's Word," go ahead and skip to week two! If you answered "video games," "pizza," "softball," "that new outfit you saw at the mall" or anything else, keep reading!

The author of this psalm knew something important: when you make it a habit to **listen to God's Word every day**, you start thinking about it all the time. And when you think about God's Word all the time, you get excited about what His Word says and want to live the way He tells you.

So how do you **make it a habit** to listen to God's Word every day?

1. ⊙ DEFINE IT. One verse a day. One chapter a day. One book of the Bible at a time (Maybe Matthew or Luke). What do you want your habit to be?

....

....

2. ⊙ CONNECT IT. Connect your new habit to an old one. Read a little before you brush your teeth or shower. What are some of your daily habits (like reading before getting out of bed in the morning or on the way to school)?

....

....

How can you connect reading God's Word with one of those habits?

....

KEEP GOING. THERE'S MORE! ⟶

DAY 5

3. ⊙ **PROTECT IT.** Protect your time reading God's Word with a plan B. What things are most likely to keep you from reading God's Word every day?

....

....

When will you read God's Word if those things get in the way?

....

4. ⊙ **STICK WITH IT.** Making a new habit takes time. Use this 30-day calendar to keep track. If you read your Bible that day, fill the box with a sticker, check mark or doodle. If you forgot, leave it blank.

SUN	MON	TUES	WED	THURS	FRI	SAT

TODAY ISN'T
ABOUT BREAKING
HABITS. IT'S ABOUT
MAKING HABITS.

HEAR

DAY 6

TWINKLE, TWINKLE LITTLE .... ,

HOW I ....

I PLEDGE ALLEGIANCE TO THE ....

OF THE ....

ROW, ROW, ROW YOUR .... ,

GENTLY ....

It's probably safe to say you were able to fill in all those blanks. Not only that, you most likely could have written the next four or five lines of each verse from memory (and added a couple of pages of Taylor Swift lyrics).

Memorizing something is easier than you think. You probably never meant to memorize those verses above but somehow you did. And it has come in very handy, hasn't it? You've been hired to perform lullabies in the local hospital, have been asked to say the Pledge at the White House, and are always there to satisfy your friends' sudden need to sing a song in the round.

Wait, no? Those verses haven't been that helpful? Well, there *are* more useful things to memorize.

I'm talking about Scripture. In Psalm 119:10-11, the psalm's author writes:

"I seek you with all my heart; do not let me stray from your commands. I have hidden your word in my heart that I might not sin against you."

When the writer of the Psalm says he has hidden God's Word in his heart, he is saying he has memorized parts of the Bible so that when he finds himself in a bad situation, he will have the words of God with him and will know what to do. Talk about handy!

So, you have a Bible. You're making it a habit to read that Bible every day. Now it's time to **listen to God's Word by memorizing it**.

"Twinkle, Twinkle, Little Star" won't be very helpful when you have to sit alone at lunch, but Jesus' words in Matthew 28:20 may be comforting.

"Row, Row, Row Your Boat" won't do you much good when you're friends are all making fun of the new kid, but if you have memorized Proverbs 13:20, you'll know what God's Word has to say about it.

Get to know God better by listening to His Word everyday. But don't just listen to it. **Memorize it**.

1. Use the index of your Bible or search feature in your Bible app to find verses that apply to situations you may face.
2. Read each verse out loud four times.
3. Write them down on index cards.
4. Place them somewhere you will look each day (like a bathroom mirror) and say them to yourself multiple times a day.

DAY 7

Grab a pen, markers or crayons and draw out one Good Idea and one Bad Idea for the following situations:

❷ YOUR FRIEND IS TAKING THE SAME MATH TEST AS YOU BUT AT A DIFFERENT TIME. HE ASKS YOU TO COPY THE QUESTIONS FROM THE TEST AND GIVE THEM TO HIM.

GOOD IDEA	BAD IDEA

❷ YOUR PARENTS TELL YOU TO CLEAN YOUR ROOM BEFORE YOU CAN GO TO YOUR FRIENDS HOUSE.

GOOD IDEA	BAD IDEA

❷ YOU SEE A GROUP OF KIDS PICKING ON SOMEONE IN THE HALLWAY.

GOOD IDEA	BAD IDEA

We all know right from wrong. It's almost as if there is a small voice in our heads telling us the difference between the good ideas and the bad ideas. God's Word tells us this is His Spirit speaking to us.

"[He] put his Spirit in our hearts as a deposit, guaranteeing what is to come" (2 Corinthians 1:22).

And a great way to get to know God is to **listen to God's Spirit**. He is in your heart, helping you make the wise choice and warning you against the bad ideas. And the more you listen to God's Spirit, the louder He becomes—the easier it is to feel and hear what He's saying.

Use this space to tell about a time you were faced with a decision and remember feeling like you knew the right choice from the wrong choice—when you could feel God's Spirit in your heart telling you what to do. If you can't think of a time, ask someone you know who has loved and followed God a while—maybe a parent, a neighbor, a teacher, or a coach.

....

....

....

....

....

....

....

....

IF YOU WANT TO KNOW GOD . . .
REMEMBER HIS WORDS.

❂ **THERE ARE LOTS OF VERSES IN THE BIBLE THAT ARE WORTH REMEMBERING. HERE ARE A FEW TO GET YOU STARTED:**

"Faith is being sure of what we hope for and certain of what we do not see."
(Hebrews 11:1)

"We are God's workmanship, created in Christ Jesus to do good works, which God prepared in advance for us to do."
(Ephesians 2:10)

"Trust in the LORD with all your heart and lean not on your own understanding; in all your ways acknowledge him, and he will make your paths straight."
(Proverbs 3:5-6)

"May the words of my mouth and the meditation of my heart be pleasing in your sight, O LORD, my Rock and my Redeemer." (Psalm 19:14)

"God so loved the world that he gave his one and only Son, that whoever believes in him shall not perish but have eternal life." (John 3:16)

Do not be anxious about anything, but in everything, by prayer and petition, with thanksgiving, present your requests to God. And the peace of God, which transcends all understanding, will guard your hearts and your minds in Christ Jesus. (Philippians 4:6-7)

WEEK 2

PRAY

PRAY

Have you ever been friends with someone you never talked to?

Didn't think so.

If you want to know someone, you talk with them. You say things and they listen. They say things and you listen. It's how we become friends.

The same is true when it comes to God. If you want to know God, pray to Him. And here's the really great news—because of Jesus, you aren't just praying to some far-off, mysterious, unknown God. You're praying to Someone who really understands.

Here's something you might not know:

Before Jesus came to earth, the Israelites—people who loved God— would connect to God through priests. The priests would regularly offer things like animals to God to make up for the bad decisions of the Israelites. Once a year, on the Day of Atonement, the High Priest would walk through a curtain into a very holy place in the temple and offer a sacrifice to God to make up for all the sins of the people.

On the day that Jesus died, actually at the exact moment Jesus died, that curtain—the one that separated the very holy place in the temple from the rest of the world—was torn. The separation between God and people was over. Jesus defeated sin and changed the way we connect with God from then on.

Now, Jesus is like our High Priest. The writer of Hebrews says it this way:

> *"We do not have a high priest who is unable to sympathize with our weaknesses, but we have one who has been tempted in every way, just as we are—yet was without sin. Let us then approach the throne of grace with confidence, so that we may receive mercy and find grace to help us in our time of need"* (Hebrews 4:15-16).

Isn't that incredible? **You connect to God through prayer** because of Jesus.

And Jesus understands what it's like to . . .
. . . live on this planet.
. . . feel hurt.
. . . be tempted.

He understands. Not only because He's God and He knows everything. He understands because He has walked on this planet and experienced life in a human body. But He did not sin. Instead, He defeated sin.

That means you can come to Him. Anytime. Anywhere. Boldly.

And because you know a little something about Jesus, you already know Who you are talking to. So, remember this: **If you want to know God, pray to Him**. Make it habit. Still not sure how to start? That's okay. This week, let's spend a little time talking about how you can pray.

DAY 1

It was Christmas Eve but Amy Scharman and her twelve brothers and sisters had no gifts under the tree. It was the first Christmas without their father and the weight of raising thirteen children alone had left Amy's mother unable to buy any gifts for Christmas.

Unexpectedly, the Scharmans heard a knock on the back door. Curious to see who could be visiting at this hour on Christmas Eve, Amy and a few of her brothers and sisters opened the door but no one was there. Instead, there were ten large bags filled with gifts for all thirteen children. Ten years later, Amy and her family still don't know who to thank for making that Christmas the most memorable of all.[1]

Some things aren't about recognition. In fact, some things should be more about the act than the attention you get for it—like giving Christmas gifts to a family who can't afford them.

Or talking to God.

Have you ever seen someone pray like it was more for attention than for God? Maybe the words were a little too perfect—too rehearsed. Maybe there was no emotion behind their words—or *too much* emotion.

Talking with God should not be a show. Instead, it should be a personal conversation with a friend. And where are you more likely to have a personal conversation with a friend? In front of a crowd of people listening to your every word? Or somewhere private where only you and your friend can hear?

In Matthew 6:6, Jesus says,

"When you pray, go into your room, close the door and pray to your Father, who is unseen. Then your Father, who sees what is done in secret, will reward you."

Prayer is your way to **connect** with God. It's your time to show that you're thankful for everything from your favorite sweatshirt to Jesus paying for your sins. It's your time to be open and honest about the things you're having trouble with and to listen to what His Spirit has to say.

You might just be surprised by what can happen when you find the space to **pray alone.**

◆ **SO, IF YOU AREN'T ALREADY THERE, GO INTO YOUR ROOM AND CLOSE THE DOOR. USE THIS TIME TO PRAY ALONE. PRAY OUT LOUD. PRAY SILENTLY. OR USE THE SPACE BELOW TO WRITE YOUR OWN PRAYER TO GOD.**

....

....

....

....

....

....

....

DAY 2

Who knows you best? A parent? A brother or sister? A friend? Think about it this way: Who knows . . .

. . . your favorite dessert?
. . . the last movie you saw?
. . . your most embarrassing moments?

❍ IS THERE SOMEONE IN YOUR LIFE WHO FINISHES YOUR SENTENCES BEFORE YOU DO? HE OR SHE ALREADY KNOWS WHAT YOU'RE THINKING BEFORE YOU SAY IT. WRITE THAT PERSON'S NAME INTO THIS CONVERSATION:

YOU: "Man, I am *so* pumped about—"

.... :   "Tell me about it! I wonder if—"

YOU: "I know! I would absolutely—"

.... :   "Freak out!"

❍ NOW, FIND THAT PERSON AND ASK THEM THESE QUESTIONS:

1. Exactly how many hairs are growing on my head?
2. What is one secret I haven't told anyone—not even you?
3. What am I thinking about right now?

Okay, don't do that. But if you did, how do you think the conversation would go? Probably not well. There are some things no one knows about you. No one except . . .

God.

That's right. God knows everything from your favorite dessert to the exact number of hairs on your head. He knows every thought, secret, and problem you have all the time.

So why do we sometimes pray to Him as if He only pays attention to us between the words "Dear God" and "Amen"?

In Matthew 6:7-8, Jesus tells His followers,

> *"When you pray, do not keep on babbling like pagans, for they think they will be heard because of their many words. Do not be like them, for your Father knows what you need before you ask him."*

Quick question. Which prayer is God more likely to listen to?

» "O dearest Heavenly Father, who art residing among the heavens, as of late I have found myself in dire need of assistance and wisdom as it pertains to the relations between myself and my mother."

» "God, help me not to fight with my mom so much."

Trick question! He hears both prayers. (Of course, one of those prayers might seem a little more normal for *you*.) Either way, God already knows you're fighting with your mom. He knows you need help studying for your test. He knows your friend is sick. So when you pray, remember you aren't **connecting** with a far-off Someone in the sky. You're **connecting** with a Father who is closer to you than your own skin. So don't pray to a God you have to impress or put on a show for—**pray to a God who knows you**.

DAY 3

⊘ DRAW A . . .

PERSON WITH SPINACH IN THEIR TEETH	PERSON WITH AN ANIMAL ABOUT TO ATTACK THEM	PERSON WITH HAIR STICKING UP (NOT ON PURPOSE)

What is the very first thing you see when you look at these pictures? What if the person in each picture was your best friend? Would you start your conversation with:

"Look out! There's an animal about to attack you!"

or . . .

"Hey, I need you to do something for me."

Hopefully, you would warn your friend of the coming danger or embarrassment before jumping right into your thing. The same is true if your friend got a great haircut or a cool new jacket. When something is that noticeable, you have to point it out first before jumping into a conversation, right?

When Jesus taught His followers how to pray, He taught them to start by pointing out the most noticeable thing about God. In Matthew 6:9, He says

"This, then, is how you should pray: 'Our Father in heaven, hallowed be your name.'"

Which is just a fancy way of saying:
"God, first things first: You *rock*! You are better, cooler, and awesome-r than anyone else in the universe!"

God made everything from the vast galaxies to the tiniest ant. He walked around on earth healing the blind, raising the dead and forever changing the way the world thought of Him. He paid the price for every sin or bad choice ever made—past, present and future.

To start a conversation with Him *without* acknowledging all that He has done would be like having a conversation with your friend and never mentioning the fact that his entire tooth is covered in dark green, slimy spinach. It's too obvious to go unmentioned.

God is great.
Better than all others.
Above anything on earth.
Hallowed.

So when you **connect** to God through prayer, start by recognizing Him for who He is. **Pray with gratitude.** ("Gratitude" just means being thankful.) Start by thanking Him for all He has done—for being such a big and powerful God.

⊘ THERE ARE COUNTLESS REASONS YOU HAVE TO BE GRATEFUL TO GOD. TAKE A MINUTE TO LIST THE TOP FIVE THINGS YOU HAVE SEEN GOD DO IN YOUR LIFE OR IN THE LIVES OF OTHERS THAT DESERVE GRATITUDE.

1. ....

2. ....

3. ....

4. ....

5. ....

DAY 4

Have you ever been so mad, frustrated, angry, or upset that you just wanted to *scream*? Maybe something happened that seemed so unfair and flat-out *wrong* that you just couldn't handle it. Maybe whatever happened was actually very fair but still something made you mad. Maybe you're feeling that way right now.

How about this? Put down this book. Find a place where no one can hear you and let out a huge, long, lung-bursting scream.

Feel better?

We all have things we need to talk about. And sometimes letting out a good healthy scream into a pillow or away from others can help. But you know what else can help? Talking to God!

That's right—praying isn't just about thanking God and asking for things. Just like a best friend, God is there to listen to your problems, too. The thing is, sometimes we think we have to come off as perfect Christians when we pray. But nothing could be further from the truth.

God wants you to be honest when you pray. He wants you to be honest about what you feel when it comes to . . .

> . . . green peas.
> . . . your math teacher.
> . . . being grounded.
> . . . your parents' divorce.

If there were ever a safe place to turn when nothing is going your way, it's to God. But God isn't just a pillow to scream in. He wants you to **pray with honesty**. He wants you to know that He is listening to you. And He wants you to know that He has a plan for you and can make good things come out of some of the worst situations.

In Matthew 6:10, Jesus continues His example of how to pray by saying,

"Your kingdom come, your will be done on earth as it is in heaven."

In other words, when you **pray with honesty**, you're handing your problems over to God. And by talking through your hatred of green peas with Him, you may just begin to understand His plan—His will—to feed your body the good food it needs to be healthy.

Sometimes (probably most of the time) you won't understand God's plan right away but when you **connect** with Him and ask that His "will be done" instead of your own plan, your attitude can change. God has everything under control and all of a sudden, it won't seem to matter as much as it did before.

A conversation with God can change how you feel completely—kind of like a good scream into your pillow.

❍ START BEING OPEN AND HONEST WITH GOD BY COMPLETING THESE SENTENCES AND PRAYING FOR HIS WILL TO BE DONE IN THESE AREAS.

1. It makes me angry when:

   ....

2. I get sad when I think about:

   ....

3. It's unfair that:

   ....

4. I don't understand why:

   ....

DAY 5

⊙ **DRAW A LINE TO MATCH THE ITEMS ON THE LEFT WITH THE RELATED ITEM ON THE RIGHT.**

PEANUT BUTTER	SOCKS
SALT	TOOTHPASTE
SUN	ROBIN
BERT	MISS PIGGY
KERMIT	JELLY
BATMAN	MOON
SHOES	COOKIES
TOOTHBRUSH	PILLOW
MILK	ERNIE
BLANKET	PEPPER

Some things just go together. Cookies aren't the same without milk. What's a peanut butter sandwich with no jelly? And Kermit would be lost without his famous, karate-kicking counterpart, Miss Piggy.

Just like each of these things needs the other, we all need God. He's our Heavenly Father. We depend on Him for everything from food to shelter to friendship.

When Jesus talked to His followers about how they should pray, His prayer began by telling God how incredible He is. Next, He asked for God's plan to happen. Then, in Matthew 6:11, He asks God to:

"Give us today our daily bread."

He asks God to give us the food we need.

But what Jesus was teaching us to ask for is so much more than cereal and sandwiches. God provides us with all kinds of basic needs each day: love, being able to make smart decisions, feeling good about ourselves—to name a few.

The problem is that it's easy to forget to ask God for stuff that's so basic. Instead we pray like we're rubbing a magic lamp. We ask God for a good grade on our test, a new video game, or for that certain someone to notice us in art class.

But Jesus made it a point to tell us to **pray for our needs** because something important happens when you ask God for what you need. No, it doesn't suddenly appear before your eyes—it reminds you just how much you depend on Him.

Chances are, if you don't ask God to give you breakfast, lunch and dinner today, you will probably still have something to eat. But you'll miss out on the awesome reminder of how great God is to provide those things for you each and every day.

> ❂ SO TAKE THIS TIME TO RECOGNIZE ALL THE IMPORTANT THINGS GOD PROVIDES FOR YOU EVERY DAY. USE THE SPACE BELOW TO DRAW A FEW OF THE BASIC NEEDS HE MEETS ON A DAILY BASIS. WHEN YOU'RE DONE, SAY A PRAYER FOR EACH ITEM YOU DREW—THAT GOD WILL CONTINUE TO PROVIDE FOR YOU AND THAT HE WILL HELP YOU TO BE MORE AWARE OF WHAT HE GIVES YOU.

PRAY

DAY 6

◑ DRAW A LINE IN THESE PICTURES TO DIVIDE THEM FAIRLY:

Pretty tough, huh?

Well, in case you haven't heard it yet from your parents, teachers and coaches:

Life's not fair.

It just isn't. There will always be a bigger piece of cake, someone with newer clothes, a person who is first in line and a person who is last.

But instead of groaning and rolling your eyes, you should be leaping for joy!

Why?

We have all made some pretty bad choices. Maybe you have lied, cheated, gossiped, or gotten *really* angry. The Bible calls those sins. But not one of us has gotten a fair punishment for our bad choices. Sure, you might have gotten grounded, lost TV privileges or stayed in at recess, but the Bible says that fair would be for you to be separated from God forever. God is perfect so sin separates us from Him. That's fair.

But that's not what has happened, is it? That's why the next part of Jesus' prayer in Mathew chapter 6 is so important. He says,

"Forgive us our debts, as we also have forgiven our debtors" (verse 12).

Forgive us just like we forgive each other.

Just a little while later, Jesus would hold up His end of the deal. He died on a cross and rose to life so that we would never have to be separated from God because of our sins. Jesus died on the cross two thousand years ago which means that He forgave all our sins before we even made them—before we were ever born!

Talk about unfair for Jesus.

But even though Jesus already forgave us, asking for His forgiveness should still be a big part of our conversations with God. When we **connect** with God and **pray for forgiveness**, we're admitting to what we've done wrong. We're telling Him that we have messed up and we need His help, not only to clean up the mess our sins made, but to remind us to give others the same forgiveness He has given us.

Forgive us for the bad choices we have made. Help us to forgive people who have hurt us. And keep us from doing those wrong things again!

So when you pray, **pray for forgiveness**. Ask for God's help to make better choices tomorrow. Pray that life stays unfair.

☻ HAVE YOU EVER MADE A REALLY BAD CHOICE? WHAT HAPPENED? DID YOU EVER ADMIT YOU WERE WRONG? TELL ABOUT IT HERE—OR JUST TELL IT TO GOD SINCE HE ALREADY KNOWS ABOUT IT ANYWAY:

....

....

....

DAY 7

Each day . . .

> . . . your heart beats over 100,000 times.

> . . . you take more than 20,000 breaths.

> . . . you blink more than 15,000 times.

But all this is going on in the background while you concentrate on things like beating your best time in Mario Kart.

In 1 Thessalonians 5:17, Paul says praying should be as constant as your heartbeat. It should come as naturally as blinking. He says to

"pray continually."

Now, that doesn't mean you're so busy praying you can't stop long enough to answer a question in your social studies class. You don't have to be in a constant conversation with God 24/7, but you should be **connected** to God 24/7. You should always be aware that He is with you.

Why do you think that is? Is it because God only loves you when you pray? Because He only tunes in when you say the words "Dear God" and immediately shuts you out after "Amen"?

No way!

God's love for you never changes. If you pray 13 times a year or 13 times a minute, God loves you the same.

God wants you to pray continually so you will feel as comfortable talking to Him as you do talking to your very best friend. But for that to be true prayer needs to be . . .

. . . more than a memorized meal-time song.

. . . more than a last-minute plea to remember the facts for your math test.

. . . more than a quick "thank You" after a big win on the field.

It's all of those things combined and then some. Being **connected** to God and **praying continually** means knowing you can turn to God anytime, anywhere, 24/7.

When you are:

excited about your birthday party,
hurt by something someone said,
or scared of not being picked for the best team in PE.

Praying is not something you have to sit down, close your eyes and fold your hands to do. You can also pray when you're walking from one class to another, when you're doing your homework or picking your nose.

God is always there to listen.

And the more you turn to God, the more you **connect** with God, the more you will know God.

Just like you have to get in the habit of reading your Bible each day, you have to get in the habit of praying continually. Start by coming up with cues to pray throughout your day. Cues could be things like before a meal, whenever a clock chimes or every time a phone buzzes.

◑ WHAT WILL BE YOUR CUES TO PRAY?

....

....

....

IF YOU WANT TO KNOW GOD . . .
PRAY TO HIM.

Remember, because of Jesus you can pray directly to God anytime, anywhere, boldly.

And when you pray, it will help you will **connect** with God.

THERE'S NO MAGIC FORMULA FOR PRAYING. BUT THERE ARE SOME THINGS YOU CAN KEEP IN MIND WHEN YOU ARE TALKING TO GOD.

"Do not be anxious about anything, but in everything, by prayer and petition, with thanksgiving, present your requests to God."
(PHILIPPIANS 4:6)

Pray with gratitude.

Pray honestly.

Pray for forgiveness.

WEEK 3

TALK

TALK

Here are two facts about you:

You like to talk about what you like.
You like to hang out with other people who talk about what you like.
Isn't that true?

Name one thing that you like to talk about: ▨▨▨▨▨▨▨

Name one person you like to talk to about that thing: ▨▨▨▨

Not only do you probably have a lot of fun talking about ▨▨▨▨

with ▨▨▨▨▨▨ , but when you do you probably

both discover more about whatever it is you both like.

Peter and John were two people who both liked to talk about Jesus.

Maybe that seems strange to you. But these were two guys who hung out with Jesus. In fact, they were in Jesus' group of friends. They knew Him well. And because they knew Jesus—they saw what Jesus did and heard what Jesus said—it made them want to talk about Him like crazy.

In fact, the book of Acts tells about this one time Peter and John got into trouble for talking about Jesus. They were standing right outside the temple saying:

> *"Salvation is found in no one else, for there is no other name under heaven given to men by which we must be saved" (Acts 4:12).*

That's pretty cool, right? Well, some of the religious leaders didn't think so. They still weren't convinced that Jesus was really who He said He was. So, they threw Peter and John in jail for the night.

The next day, the religious leaders told Peter and John they could go as long as they promised to stop talking about Jesus.

What do you think they said?

Well, they didn't agree of course! Instead they said:

> **"We cannot help speaking about what we have seen and heard"** (Acts 4:20).

That's pretty amazing. You've probably felt that way before. Like you just can't stop talking about something even if you tried. That's how Peter and John felt.

They had heard Jesus teach amazing things. They had seen Jesus work incredible miracles. And most of all, they were there when Jesus was crucified on the cross, and then they saw Him alive three days later! Who wouldn't talk about that?

Okay, it might be easier for those guys to talk about Jesus. After all, they did walk around with Him for a few years.

But you know something about Jesus, too. You know what He has done in your life and the way that He has used others to help you learn more about Him and His love for you. That's something about Jesus that no one else knows—unless you talk about it.

The same is true for other people. They know what Jesus has done in their lives. So when you talk about Him together, you both get to see something new about who He is. It's like God wants us to learn more about Him by talking with other people about what He's done. So here's the one thing to remember: if you want to know God, talk about him with your friends.

If you want to know more about how to do that, you're in luck. That's what this week is all about.

DAY 1

Before you start reading today, find a ball and glove. Go outside and play catch by yourself.

Not very fun, is it?

What would happen if you tried to play football alone? Or started a Ping-Pong match on your own?

Some things just don't work when you are the only one doing them. Knowing and following God is one of those things. If you want to keep getting to know God better, it's important to hang around other people who know God—to talk with other people who believe in Jesus.

Hebrews 10:25 says,

> *"Let us not give up meeting together, as some are in the habit of doing, but let us encourage one another."*

These words were written to some of the first people who believed in Jesus. Christianity was still a new idea, but meeting and talking with other people who followed and loved Jesus too helped them **see** . . .

. . . Jesus was God.
. . . God loved them.
. . . God wanted them to love *everyone*.

Now, this doesn't mean we *only* hang around other believers. It's important to talk with all kinds of people—Jesus certainly did! But it's also important to make sure you take time during your week to **talk with people who believe in Jesus**.

Just think, if you were training for a big Ping-Pong tournament but you couldn't find anyone to play Ping-Pong with, you wouldn't get any better, would you? But if a few of your friends were professional Ping-Pong players, I bet you'd get really good really fast!

TALK

The same is true about having a relationship with God. In order to know God better, you have to be around other people who know God.

King Solomon knew this was true. Just listen to these wise words from the book of Proverbs:

"He who walks with the wise grows wise, but a companion of fools suffers harm" (Proverbs 13:20).

It just makes sense that you'll care about what your friends care about. When you hang around wise people and **talk with people who believe in Jesus**, you get to know God better.

USE THE SPACE BELOW TO MAKE A LIST OF PEOPLE YOU KNOW WHO HAVE A STRONG FAITH IN GOD. HAVING FAITH IN GOD MEANS BELIEVING IN HIM AND TRUSTING HIM. WHO DO YOU LOOK UP TO? WHO IS A GOOD EXAMPLE OF WHAT IT LOOKS LIKE TO HAVE A RELATIONSHIP WITH GOD? NEXT TO EACH NAME, WRITE A FEW TRAITS THAT YOU ADMIRE IN EACH OF THESE PEOPLE. (Maybe they're honest, kind, generous, or compassionate, etc.)

DAY 2

Who knows you best? Find those people and ask them the following questions about yourself:

1. What is one thing I am really good at?
2. What is my best subject in school?
3. What is my favorite book?
4. What is the best thing about my personality?
5. What is one thing I could work harder on?

When you know and care about someone, you're able to talk about what makes that person special. The people who know you best probably talk about the things they know and love about you. In the same way, it's important to talk with people who know God about the things they know and love about Him.

In Matthew chapter 16, Jesus asked His disciples,

"Who do people say that I am?"

His friends shared what they had heard from people who didn't know Jesus very well. But what Jesus really wanted to know was what His friends thought about Him—the people who knew Him best. So, He asked them:

"What about you? . . . Who do you say I am?"

Without a doubt, Peter said He was the Son of God. Peter and the disciples had been with Jesus, seen His miracles, and heard His teaching. Peter knew without a doubt He was who He said He was: God on earth.

So when you talk to other believers, **talk about who God is**.

Learn from those who know Him best by talking about . . .

. . . how He might feel about what is going on in your life.
. . . what His plans are for you and the rest of the world.
. . . how He helps others.

Right now, you may only **see** God as Someone to go to when you really, really, *really* want that new Xbox or when you have looked *everywhere* (yes, including the freezer) for your library book—and if you don't find it soon, your mom is gonna be *ticked*.

You can definitely turn to God in those times, but He is so much more than that. That's why it's important to talk to other people who know and love God about how *they* **see** Him.

DON'T STOP YET.
THERE'S MORE!

→

TALK

WHO I THINK GOD IS:

WHO OTHER PEOPLE THINK GOD IS:

GOD IS...

GOD IS...

GOD IS...

GOD IS...

GOD IS...

GOD IS...

GOD IS...

GOD IS...

GOD IS...

GOD IS...

STILL DAY 2

 USE THE SPACE TO THE LEFT TO WRITE FIVE WORDS TO DESCRIBE WHO YOU THINK GOD IS. THEN, ASK A FEW OF THE PEOPLE FROM THE LIST YOU MADE YESTERDAY TO DESCRIBE WHO THEY THINK GOD IS. WRITE THEIR ANSWERS IN THE SPACE PROVIDED.

When you're finished, write each word in a square of this grid. Cut out the squares and put them in places you are sure to see each day. (Maybe someplace like the refrigerator door, your mirror, above your bed, your math notebook, etc.)

TALK

DAY 3

It's Saturday afternoon. The sun is high in the sky. There's not a cloud for a hundred miles. You have your red baseball uniform on and you're standing over home plate holding your lucky bat.

The championship game your team has worked so hard to play in is finally here and the pressure is on. You're surrounded by players wearing the other team's colors: grey and black. The bleachers on the other side of the diamond are full of jeering fans waving black flags. Your eyes swing to the bleachers closest to you expecting to see them full of friends and family waving cheerful red flags.

But they are completely empty.

Not one single person showed up to cheer your team on to the championship. Not your parents. Not your friends. Not even Ricky's dad who shouts until his face matches the red flag in his hand.

You are all alone.

Sometimes being in a relationship with God can feel this way. You may feel like you are the only one who . . .

> . . . prays in the cafeteria before lunch.
> . . . doesn't talk badly about the school bully.
> . . . shows respect to your teachers.

That's why Hebrews 3:13 tells us to "encourage one another daily." As Christians, it's important to encourage other believers. But how do you do that?

Talk about what God says.

While Jesus was here on earth, He said some incredible things. And when you talk with each other about those incredible words, it helps everyone **see** who God is and why it's important to keep following Him.

WHEN YOU SEE SOMEONE . . .

> . . . being nice to a bully
> . . . taking care of someone in need
> . . . sharing about their relationship with God
> . . . giving away their last cupcake
> . . . forgiving someone who has hurt them
> . . . getting help to break up a fight
> . . . keeping their promises

YOU CAN ENCOURAGE THEM BY REMINDING THEM THAT JESUS SAYS . . .

> . . . love your enemies (Matthew 5:44).
> . . . whatever you do for others, you do for Him (Matthew 25:40).
> . . . love God with all your heart, mind and soul (Matthew 22:37).
> . . . love others as much as you love yourself (Matthew 22:39).
> . . . forgive others and God will forgive you (Matthew 6:14).
> . . . those who make peace will be called sons of God (Matthew 5:9).
> . . . do not break the promises you have made (Matthew 5:33).

Just like bleachers full of cheering fans go crazy when you hit a home run, we should be building each other up everyday by **talking about what God says.**

This next week, make a goal to encourage one person each day with Jesus' words. Whether it's someone you see doing the right thing or a friend who is down, **talking about what God says** just might be the kind of cheering on they need.

⊙ **EACH OF THE VERSES ABOVE ARE WORDS STRAIGHT FROM JESUS' MOUTH. LOOK THEM UP IN YOUR BIBLE, ON A BIBLE APP OR WEBSITE. READ DIFFERENT VERSIONS OF EACH VERSE AND CHOOSE THE ONE THAT YOU UNDERSTAND BEST. WRITE EACH VERSE ON A CARD AND GIVE THE CARDS TO SOME OF YOUR FRIENDS AND FAMILY THIS WEEK TO ENCOURAGE THEM TO KEEP DOING THE RIGHT THING.**

TALK

DAY 4

There are some things you just shouldn't say out loud.

> "I really need to burp."
> "Have you stopped wetting the bed yet?"
> "I like the way my boogers taste."
> "What's *Star Wars*?"

Then there are things you can only say to people you know and trust.

> "Is there anything in my teeth?"
> "I am really scared of the dark."
> "I hope my dad doesn't marry her."
> "I feel like I don't have any friends."
> "Is God really good all the time?"

Everyone has doubts and questions about God's Story. It's a natural part of figuring out who God is. And if you want to really know God, the best thing to do is **talk about your doubts and questions** with people you know and trust.

If it feels like everyone in your life expects you to have it all figured out, listen to this verse:

"Be merciful to those who doubt" (Jude 1:22).

A man named Jude wrote this letter to Christians all over the world in the years right after Jesus lived. He was telling the Christians that people would have questions and doubts about the story of God. And when those people asked their questions or had doubts, they were to show them mercy.

TALK

Mercy = compassion, kindness, sympathy, understanding.

This is how everyone who knows God should treat your doubts and questions. And this is how you should respond to the doubts and questions other people bring to you. As Christians, it's important to find safe people to talk with about what you think you can't say out loud.

If you keep your doubts and questions to yourself, you will always have something in the back of your mind keeping you from really getting to know God. But when you **talk about your doubts and questions** with other people who know and love God, you start to **see** a little more of who God is.

⊘ **WHAT ARE SOME DOUBTS AND QUESTIONS ABOUT GOD YOU HAVE OR HAVE HEARD FROM OTHERS?**

....

....

....

⊘ **THIS WEEK, FIND SOMEONE WHO HAS A GREAT RELATIONSHIP WITH GOD AND TALK THROUGH THE DOUBTS AND QUESTIONS YOU WROTE ABOVE.**

DAY 5

☉ WHAT ARE YOUR THREE FAVORITE MEMORIES? (THEY COULD BE WITH FAMILY, YOUR BEST FRIEND OR SOMETHING THAT HAPPENED TO YOU ALL ALONE.)

1.

....

2.

....

3.

....

It's always fun to tell stories like this. Thinking back and sharing great memories can make anyone happy, whether it's remembering when you won the championship, the day you found a $50 bill in your backyard, or that time your dad picked you up from school wearing his Bugs Bunny slippers. (Wait, scratch that. You're still trying to forget that last one.)

The point is, talking about cool memories is a great way to connect with other people. It's also a great way to **see** who God is. God has done some pretty incredible things and when you **talk about what He's done**, it helps us all remember just how amazing God is.

In 1 Chronicles 16, King David sings a song to celebrate bringing something very important to God—the Ark of the Covenant—back to Jerusalem. In his song, David sings:

"Remember the wonders he has done" (1 Chronicles 16:12).

Things hadn't always been easy for David. When he felt discouraged, he often wrote songs. In these songs, David remembered the great things God had done for him. He tells us to do the same: to remember and **talk about what He's done**.

When you have doubts . . .
When you feel all alone . . .
When it seems like God doesn't even care . . .

. . . talk about what He's done.

He created the entire universe.
He parted the Red Sea.
He rescued the Israelites from slavery.
He healed the sick, fed the hungry and calmed the storms.
He raised Jesus from the dead so we could be with Him forever.

It's easy to get so focused on what's going on in our own lives that we forget all the wonderful things God has done. But when it feels like God can't handle your problems, **talk about what He's done**. We worship an awesome, powerful God and if He can cover every square inch of Egypt in slimy, squirmy frogs, He can probably get your dad to invest in some new slippers.

Ɔ   ENCOURAGE EACH OTHER THIS WEEK BY TALKING ABOUT THE AMAZING THINGS GOD HAS DONE. WRITE OR DRAW SOME OF THOSE HERE:

TALK

DAY 6

◔ **TAKE A FEW MINUTES AND DRAW HOW YOU WOULD USE EACH OF THESE ITEMS:**

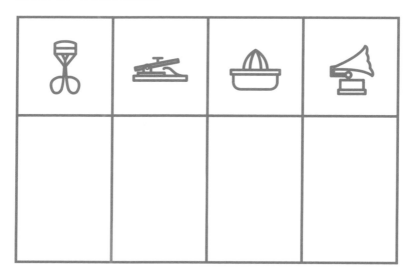

Some of those were pretty hard! But I bet you came up with creative ways to use each one.

Imagine this: You walk into your friend's room to find he is using his brand new Xbox as a bookend. He is using his iPod as a paperweight. And the tablet he got for Christmas is serving as a coaster, soaked in large beads of water.

You would think, "What is he *doing*?? Someone needs to tell him what those things are capable of!"

Our relationship with God can be the same way. Unless we talk with other people who know God about what God is doing in their lives, we might completely miss out on knowing some of the incredible things God can do. And just like your friend who thinks a tablet is simply a coaster, you might think God is simply a wish-granter. But when you talk about what's He's doing in the lives of the people around you, you'll see that God is so much bigger than you ever imagined! You'll begin to understand more of the radical, life-changing, world-rocking things He has in store for your life!

Romans 1:12 says that when people talk about what God has been doing in their lives, they can be, "mutually encouraged by each other's faith."

The early Christians knew that when you share your faith, or **talk about what He's doing**, you hear stories from real people who have felt and **seen** what God can do. Each of those stories allows you to **see** a bigger picture of who God is.

If you take the time to talk about what God is doing in the lives of your friends and family, you may learn that . . .

. . . God comforts Dexter when he's scared.
. . . God reminds Mary only to say kind words.
. . . God gives Marcus the determination to finish his homework.

When you hear how God is working in the lives of others, you start to **see** ways God can work in your own life.

KEEP GOING. THERE'S MORE!

TALK

STILL DAY 6

⊙ **ANSWER THE FOLLOWING QUESTIONS IN THE SPACE PROVIDED. WHEN YOU'RE DONE, LOOK BACK AT THAT LIST OF PEOPLE YOU WROTE THE FIRST DAY OF THIS WEEK— THE LIST OF PEOPLE YOU WANT TO HANG AROUND. PICK A FEW OF THOSE PEOPLE AND ASK THEM THE FOLLOWING QUESTIONS. WRITE THEIR ANSWERS ON A SEPARATE PIECE OF PAPER AND SHARE YOUR OWN ANSWERS WITH THEM!**

What is one new thing you have discovered in God's Story lately?

....

....

What is one thing you feel like God wants you to do or say this week?

....

....

How has God answered prayers for you?

....

....

What are you praying for now?

....

....

WHEN YOU HEAR
HOW GOD IS WORKING
IN THE LIVES OF
OTHERS, YOU START
TO SEE WAYS GOD CAN
WORK IN
YOUR OWN LIFE.

TALK

DAY 7

❂ WHAT ARE THE BEST GIFTS YOU HAVE EVER GOTTEN?

....

....

When you got those presents, what did you do? (After squealing like a little girl and jumping for joy, of course.)

You probably ripped open the packaging, made sure it was as awesome as you imagined it would be and bragged about it to all your friends.

Believe it or not, things haven't changed in over 2,000 years. Jesus' disciple, Peter, told the first Christians what to do when they got the best gift anyone could ask for: the hope that comes with being a follower of Jesus.

How is that better than the gifts you listed above, you ask? It's better because you have the hope to make it through anything. You know that the God who made you and loves you is in control, and that He will work everything out in the end.

Peter told those who had just received this hope in their lives to keep Jesus first, numero uno, top dog. Then he said to be ready to **talk with anyone who asks** about Jesus. (After squealing like a little girl, I assume.)

> *"In your hearts set apart Christ as Lord. Always be prepared to give an answer to everyone who asks you to give the reason for the hope that you have. But do this with gentleness and respect"* (1 Peter 3:15).

Check out those last three words: *gentleness and respect.*

We all know people who don't have the hope and joy that come with knowing God. But do you think they will be more likely to want to know God if you make them feel worthless or if you talk about your faith with **gentleness and respect**?

"When you know God, it shows. You will treat others with respect. You will make wiser choices. You will turn to God in all situations."

People will want to **see** God the way you **see** Him. People will ask. So be ready to **talk with anyone who asks**.

❂ **TAKE A MINUTE TO ANSWER THESE QUESTIONS WITH GENTLENESS AND RESPECT:**

"Why does your family go to church?"

....

"Why do you pray before you eat?"

....

"Why do you read your Bible?"

....

"Why do you believe in God?"

....

"Why are you so nice to people?"

....

Use this space to write the answer(s) to any question(s) you have already been asked or think you could be asked:

Question: ....

Answer: ....

IF YOU WANT TO KNOW GOD . . .
TALK ABOUT HIM WITH YOUR FRIENDS.

Before you talk to other people about God, it might help for you to take some time to think about what God has done in your life. What is your story? How has God shown up in your life to show you more about who He is and how much He loves you?

❂ WRITE YOUR STORY—THE STORY OF THE WAYS GOD HAS SHOWN UP IN YOUR LIFE—HERE:

When and how did you first believe God's story?

How has God changed your life?

How has God answered prayers for you?

What has God taught you?

And you know what? These questions could be great to ask your friends and family, too! You never know what you might learn about God when you **talk about Him with your friends**.

WEEK 4

LIVE

LIVE

Has someone ever given you a gift or done something for you that was so unbelievably, stinking amazing that you just had to do something big to thank them—to let them know how grateful you really were?

⊘ **GO AHEAD. NAME THE BIGGEST THING SOMEONE HAS GIVEN YOU OR DONE FOR YOU:**

When it comes to God, has God done more for you, or have you done more for God? (That answer is pretty easy to figure out.)

Paul, who wrote the book of Romans, talks a little bit about this. In Romans 11:35-36 he basically says:

Here's the thing: Did you do something so incredible for God that He is trying to find a way to thank you? No! It's the other way around. God has done everything for you. He made you. He sent His Son so you could be forgiven and made new again. Pretty much everything about you has been made for Him and Him alone.

You were made for God.

That's a big thought. It means that everything about you is designed to respond to Him. You were created so that you could show God's awesomeness to the whole world. You were made to make Him known. We all were.

Don't believe me?

Think about this. There's something inside all of us that wants to worship (to celebrate and get really excited about something). We want to get so wrapped up in something that everyone around us sees our excitement and gets excited, too.

Maybe you have felt this way about . . .
. . . a movie
. . . a basketball team
. . . a new band.

But here's what Paul was pointing out: If you have the urge to worship— to get over-the-top excited about something—why not worship the most important thing? The thing you were actually made to worship? Why not worship Jesus?

In Romans, Paul was saying: when you think about what Jesus has done for you, you realize your whole life should be spent worshiping Him.

That doesn't mean you have to spend every waking moment singing worship songs, creating artwork, dancing, or playing music for God. At some point, you're probably going to want to stop to eat a meal, take a nap, maybe play a video game. And God's okay with that.

What Paul was saying is that as you get to know God more, you may find that you want to do something just to thank Him for being awesome. You might want to find a way to honor Him with your life.

That's what worship means. It means that you will develop habits of praising and serving and giving. Because you understand that you were . . .
. . . made by God
. . . remade through Jesus
. . . made for the purpose of worshiping Him.

There's one more thing you may want to know about worship: the more you do it, the more you want to do it, and the more the people around you will catch on.

If you still aren't sure about worship, that's okay. That's what the rest of this week is about. But for now, remember this: if you want to know more about God, make him more important than anything.

DAY 1

Love.

Does that word make you starry-eyed or sick to your stomach? Sigh dreamily or feel like a thousand tarantulas are crawling over your skin? Like it or not, I bet you use the "L word" every day.

"I *love* Fridays." "I *love* chicken nuggets." "I *love* turtles."

> **GO AHEAD AND WRITE A FEW OF THOSE THINGS DOWN. WHAT DO YOU SAY THAT YOU LOVE?**

....

....

....

Of course, the word "love" means so much more than how you feel about chicken nuggets. It's more than candy hearts and sitting in a tree.

Love is . . .

. . . kind.
. . . self*less*.
. . . patient.
. . . hopeful.
. . . forgiving.
. . . generous.
. . . encouraging.
. . . understanding.

. . . *no matter what.*

During His time on earth, Jesus gave us a short list of what to love. (Surprisingly, chicken nuggets didn't make the list.)

" 'Love the Lord your God with all your heart and with all your soul and with all your mind.' This is the first and greatest commandment. And the second is like it: 'Love your neighbor as yourself.' All the Law and Prophets hang on these two commandments" **(Matthew 22:37-40).**

First, love God.
Then, love yourself.
Finally, love everyone else as much as you love yourself.

If you do those three things, you've got it covered. It's that simple. **Honor God with love.**

If you love God, you will worship Him. You will set aside time for Him. If you love yourself, you won't be jealous. You will be content. If you love others, you won't lie, cheat, steal or gossip. You will treat everyone with respect.

But it's not that simple is it? Love is such a huge part of **honoring** God . . . but it's easy to forget sometimes.

God is the most awesome thing ever . . . until you see that Bieber concert. You feel really great about yourself . . . until your hair does that peacock thing. You love everyone . . . except that kid who chose you last in P.E.

Knowing God and showing Him **honor** in your daily life means loving *no matter what.* Jesus said it was *the* most important thing we could do. We **honor God with our love** for God, ourselves and others.

◑ COME UP WITH ONE WAY TO SHOW LOVE TO . . .

GOD: ....

YOURSELF: ....

OTHERS: ....

And maybe every time you confess your undying "love" for something like chicken nuggets, remind yourself of what that word really means and the three things Jesus wants you to love.

DAY 2

Have you ever . . .

. . . sneezed without moving a muscle or making a sound?
. . . felt the itch of a mosquito bite without scratching it?
. . . seen someone yawn without yawning yourself? (there's a good chance just reading the word yawn made you yawn.

Some things are almost impossible to do without a physical response, without moving your body or making a sound.

❍ TAKE A MINUTE TO WRITE WHAT YOUR RESPONSE WOULD BE TO THE FOLLOWING THINGS:

Seeing a hairy spider the size of your fist:

....

Grape juice spewing from your mom's nose:

....

Stepping on a Lego piece with your bare foot:

....

Just like laughing out loud can make you wet your pants a little, thinking about all that God has done for us can make us want to jump up and down, dance, sing and rock out.

And we aren't alone! Thousands of years ago, the psalmist had the same response to the incredible things God had done. He wrote a song that the people would sing at God's temple. In Psalm 95:1-2, he wrote:

"Come, let us sing for joy to the Lᴏʀᴅ; let us shout aloud to the Rock of our salvation. Let us come before him with thanksgiving and extol him with music and song."

God protected the Israelites. He rescued them from slavery. He fed them in the wilderness. He gave them a new home—even when they weren't so good at obeying Him. God was always with His people and that made them want to shout for joy! It made them want to **honor God with praise.**

One great way to honor God with the way you live is to **praise Him** when you think of all He's done. You can praise God at church, at school, at home or anywhere else. You can praise God by singing, dancing, leaping to your feet or bowing low to the ground.

❷ WHAT ARE SOME THINGS GOD HAS DONE THAT MAKE YOU WANT TO PRAISE HIM?

....

....

....

❷ HOW DO YOU SHOW GOD THE JOY YOU FEEL WHEN YOU THINK ABOUT ALL HE HAS DONE?

....

....

....

❷ TAKE FIVE MINUTES TO PRAISE AND HONOR GOD IN THAT WAY NOW.

....

....

DAY 3

Which came first: the chicken or the egg?

The egg had to be first. Because all chickens come from eggs. But then where did the first egg come from? A chicken? And if that's true, where did that chicken come from? An egg? And if that's true . . .

Okay, okay. Snap out of it. You already know the answer to that one: whichever one God created first.

Now think about this: Does God love you because you obey Him? Or do you obey God because He loves you?

While you're thinking, check out these words written by Jesus' disciple, John:

> **"We know that we have come to know [God] if we obey his commands" (1 John 2:3).**

Basically, when we know God and how much He loves us, we want to obey the things He's asked us to do (or not do).

So you choose to honor God with obedience because He loves you.

You may not understand *why* God said to listen to your mom and dad but you know God. You know He cares about you even more than you care about yourself. And if He has asked you to do something, there has to be a pretty good reason.

And when you choose to obey, you can **honor God with obedience**.

It's not something He *makes* us do. We have a choice. It doesn't change how much He loves us. His love stays the same. Obeying God is simply a way of saying, "God, I trust Your love for me *so much* that I am going to do what You ask me to do—even if I don't understand why."

◑ HERE ARE JUST A FEW THINGS GOD'S WORD TELLS US TO DO. SOME WILL BE EASIER FOR YOU TO OBEY THAN OTHERS. RATE EACH VERSE WITH A 1, 2 OR 3.

1 = EASY FOR ME!
2 = SOMETIMES EASY. SOMETIMES HARD.
3 = HARD FOR ME!

1 2 3   Love God more than anything else. (Exodus 20:3-5)

1 2 3   Respect your mom and dad. (Exodus 20:12)

1 2 3   Don't hate others. (Exodus 20:13, 1 John 3:15)

1 2 3   Don't steal. (Exodus 20:15)

1 2 3   Tell the truth. (Exodus 20:16)

1 2 3   Don't be jealous of someone else. (Exodus 20:17)

1 2 3   Love your enemies. (Matthew 5:44)

1 2 3   Treat people fairly. (Micah 6:8)

1 2 3   Be humble. (Micah 6:8)

1 2 3   Think and talk about good things. (Philippians 4:8)

1 2 3   Tell others about God. (Matthew 28:19)

◑ WRITE THE ONES WITH A "3" ON A PIECE OF PAPER AND TAPE IT TO THE DOOR OF YOUR ROOM. BEFORE YOU LEAVE EACH MORNING, READ THROUGH THE VERSES AND DECIDE TO HONOR GOD WITH OBEDIENCE.

....

....

....

DAY 3

❂ WHAT IS THE BEST GIFT YOU HAVE EVER GIVEN? FIND A PICTURE OF THAT GIFT IN A MAGAZINE, ON A WEBSITE OR TAKE A PICTURE TO PRINT AND GLUE IT IN THE BOX. THEN TELL HOW IT FELT TO GIVE THAT GIFT AWAY.

Sometimes giving is just as exciting as getting something yourself. And here's the good news:

You don't have to wait until Christmas, Mother's Day or Teacher Appreciation Week to give something away!

Take a look around your house.

If you have cans of pumpkin, green beans and cranberry sauce left over from holiday feasts, check out this fact: **one in six Americans don't have enough to eat.**

If a thick winter coat from last year is taking up space in the back of your closet, think about the coldest nights of the year and consider this: **1.6 million children in America don't have anywhere to live.**

If you just bought that video game you've been saving for and your piggy bank is still heavy with coins, think about this: **Almost 50 million Americans don't have enough money to live on.**

And that's just in the United States—one of the top ten richest countries in the world! So what can you do? Decide to **honor God by being generous!** Because not only does giving something to someone feel good, it's a great way to **honor** God with the way you live.

The Bible says:

> *"If anyone has material possessions and sees his brother in need but has no pity on him, how can the love of God be in him?" (1 John 3:17).*

KEEP GOING. THERE'S MORE!

WHEN YOU KNOW
GOD AND
UNDERSTAND JUST
HOW MUCH LOVE HE
HAS FOR YOU, YOU'LL
WANT TO SHOW
OTHERS THAT LOVE.

STILL DAY 4

When you know God and understand just how much love He has for you, you'll want to show others that love. And part of that means looking around for chances to **honor God with generosity**. You can meet someone else's needs by . . .

. . . giving groceries to a local food bank.
. . . volunteering with a parent or friends at a local homeless shelter.
. . . sharing your lunch with a student who forgot theirs.
. . . lending a spare pencil to a classmate who doesn't have one.
. . . raising money to donate to a charity you believe in.

If you don't think you have something you can give right now, make a plan. Come up with a way to earn some extra cash to save up and donate, or even find a way to share your stuff (loaning your bike) and time (help with a community project).

◑ ASK A PARENT TO HELP YOU RESEARCH A FEW ORGANIZATIONS THAT GIVE TO PEOPLE IN NEED. LIST SOME OF YOUR FAVORITES HERE:

....

....

....

◑ COME UP WITH A WAY YOU CAN HELP ONE OF THOSE ORGANIZATIONS AND WRITE YOUR PLAN HERE:

....

....

....

DAY 5

Would you rather . . .

. . . your brother say "I love you" *or* do your chores for you?
. . . your parents tell you how smart you are *or* spend time helping you with your homework?
. . . your friend compliment your bag *or* carry all your things to the bus for you?

It's nice to hear kind words but sometimes actions speak louder than words. Sometimes it means a lot more when you take the time to *do something* for someone. In the Bible, the book of 1 John says:

> **"Let us not love with words or tongue but with actions and in truth" (1 John 3:18).**

Living your life to worship God is all about *doing* something for God that shows just how much you appreciate what He has done for you—putting your love for Him into *action*. But how do you **serve** God? You can't exactly hold a door open for Him or make Him breakfast. But check out these words Jesus said while He was here on earth:

> **"Whatever you did for one of the least of these brothers of mine, you did for me" (Matthew 25:40).**

How cool is that?! You may not be able to make breakfast for God but you can **honor God by serving others**. And Jesus said that whatever you do for your family, friends or complete strangers, you are doing for Him.

When you . . .
. . . help clean up after a friend's birthday party . . .
. . . volunteer in a local retirement home . . .
. . . or shovel snow for your neighbor . . .

. . . you are also helping, volunteering and shoveling snow for Jesus. He loves every person in the world so much that He died for them—

every single one of them. So when you take the time to serve the people God loves, you are worshiping and honoring God with the way you live.

❷ TAKE A FEW MINUTES TO WALK AROUND YOUR HOUSE OR NEIGHBORHOOD. FIND A WAY TO HONOR GOD BY SERVING SOMEONE. THEN, COME BACK AND DRAW A PICTURE OF WHAT YOU DID OR DRAW THE NAME OF THE PERSON YOU HELPED IN YOUR FAVORITE COOL LETTERING.

❷ WHICH DO YOU THINK MEANT MORE: YOUR ACTIONS OR IF YOU HAD ONLY SAID A FEW KIND WORDS? WHY?

....

....

....

❷ WHAT ARE SOME OTHER WAYS YOU CAN THINK OF TO SERVE THE PEOPLE GOD LOVES? (Remember . . . that includes everyone!)

....

....

....

DAY 6

Let's be honest for a minute.

If your teacher never collected homework, would you still do it?
If your mom never noticed your clean room, would you still clean it?
If there were no winners in a game, would you still practice?

We all work *for* something or someone.

A good grade.
A thumbs up.
A big, shiny trophy.

But if all those things disappeared, if no one noticed your hard work, what would you do?

In his letter to the church in Colossae, the apostle Paul said:

> **"Whatever you do, work at it with all your heart, as working for the Lord, not for men" (Colossians 3:23).**

In other words, whether you're cleaning your room or learning math, **honor God with your work**. You may not always be recognized for your hard work. Some things you do will go unnoticed. But they won't get past God. He sees your work. And no matter how big or small the job may be, God wants you to work at it as if it's the most important job in His big story.

Practice your musical instrument as if you're playing a concert for God.
Pay attention in school as if God was teaching you fractions.
Clear the table as if you were washing the very plate God had eaten His dinner on.

Every job in the world is important to God's big story. And when you work at everything you do with all your heart, you're worshipping God with your life. You are **honoring God with your work.**

So even though you might not always get a big thumbs-up or a shiny trophy, God sees your hard work and He is honored when you worship Him with everything you do.

◑ MAKE A LIST OF YOUR "JOBS" AT HOME, SCHOOL AND IN YOUR COMMUNITY.

....

....

....

◑ TAKE A FEW MINUTES TO PRAY ABOUT THESE JOBS. TELL GOD YOU WANT TO DO THESE JOBS FOR HIM. ASK GOD TO HELP YOU BE HAPPY KNOWING THAT HE MAY BE THE ONLY ONE WHO FINDS JOY IN YOUR HARD WORK.

DAY 7

Do you hear something? What's that noise? Music playing? People talking? TV blasting? No matter where we are, it seems like there's always some noise.

But try this: Go find a quiet place where you can be completely alone with God. Sit perfectly still and think about . . .

> . . . the things God has made.
> . . . what God has done for you.
> . . . what you know about God from the Bible.

◐ TRY IT FOR ONE WHOLE MINUTE.

Ready? Set? Go.

Now, give yourself a big pat on the back. You have just completed the seventh and final way to worship God with your life!

Well, almost.

Let's back up for a minute. Have you ever known someone who talks *too* much? Have you ever had a friendship that felt all about the other person and none about you?

Doesn't make a great relationship, does it?

Sometimes our relationships with God can be the same way.

"God, bless this food. Thanks. Bye."
"God, You're awesome. Thanks. Bye."
"God, help my friend feel better. Thanks. Bye."

We are so busy *living* and *doing* that we don't take the time to stop and rest—to focus on Him.

God does incredible things each and every day and if we don't stop to just focus on Him, we may miss a great chance to honor Him.

Psalm 46:10 says,

> *"Be still, and know that I am God."*

Be still. Rest. Think about God. **Honor God with rest**.

The Bible tells us to take one whole day and do nothing but rest. And it's a great goal for all of us to have. To spend one whole day each week **honoring God while we rest**. But if you're new to this whole rest idea, start with ten minutes each day. Find a time before you leave for school, after you get home or right before bed when you can go somewhere private, away from any distractions (human or electronic), sit still and think about who God is.

○ WHEN IS THE BEST TIME FOR YOU TO HONOR GOD WITH REST?

....

....

....

○ WHERE CAN YOU GO TO REST AND THINK ABOUT GOD?

....

....

....

IF YOU WANT TO KNOW GOD . . .
MAKE HIM MORE IMPORTANT THAN ANYTHING.

Worship can be pretty personal.

....

Some people like to worship God by singing loudly to God with their arms up in the air. Other people prefer to worship God by being very quiet.

....

Some people like to worship God with lots and lots of other people. Others prefer to worship God by walking alone outside where they can see nature.

....

Some people like to dance or play an instrument to worship God. Others may find that they worship God best when they are running or playing sports.

....

Some people like to worship God by giving their money or their things to people who really need them.

....

Some people like to worship God by using their time and talents to serve others.

....

There are many, many ways to honor God with your worship.

❍ WHAT ARE SOME OF THE WAYS THAT YOU WORSHIP
GOD BEST?